Contents

Mexico: Unpacked

Welcome to Mexico, on the 'bridge' between North and South America! This long, mountainous country is eight times the size of the UK, and equally BIG in personality. Head this way to find fiery volcanoes, spooky celebrations, deadly jaguars and some of the BEST beaches and WORST traffic jams in the world. The Mexicans like to say that a piece of you will never leave — so let's unpack and see if that's true!

Mexico

Fact file

Area: 1,964,375 sq km

Population: 120,286,655 (July 2014 est.)

Capital city: Mexico City

Land borders: 4,353km with three countries

Currency: Mexican peso

Main language: Spanish

Colorado River

United States of America

Baja Peninsula

Rio Bravo

Sierra Madre Occidental

Chihuahua

Sierra Madre Oriental

Gulf of California

Mexico

Gulf of Mexico

Cancún

Chichen Itza

Guadalajara

Mexico City

Puebla

• Pico de Orizaba

Sierra Madre del Sur

• Oaxaca

Pacific
Ocean

Belize

Guatemala

You can see on this map how Mexico's longest river, the Rio Bravo, forms a natural border with the United States. Mexico's capital city, Mexico City is shown too, along with some of the other places you will discover in this book.

Look out for the world's widest tree, a type of cypress. It takes about 30 people with arms outstretched to reach the 54m around its trunk!

Mexican has a young, dynamic population – about half are under 30 years old.

Viva Mexico!

Only ten countries in the world have a bigger population than Mexico. Some of the earliest people to live here were among the most advanced, creative and bloodthirsty of their time! From the ground-breaking Mayans to fearless Spanish conquerers, everyone in history made their mark. Now Mexico has a high-flying modern society, and a magical mix of cultures too.

NO WAY!

The descendants of the Aztecs speak a language called Nahuatl. Some of its words have passed into English – including tomatoes (tomatl) and chocolate (chocolatl)!

The Olmecs carved huge heads out of boulders. Some are taller than an adult and weigh over 40 tonnes!

Great Civilizations

Beginning with the Olmecs in about 1500 BCE, some great civilizations grew up in Mexico. The Aztecs arrived in the 1300s, believing they would find their home when they saw an eagle perched on a cactus holding a snake. According to legend, this actually happened – on Lake Texcoco in central Mexico! It became the site of their capital city, Tenochtitlán.

Spanish Conquest

In 1519, Spanish Conquistador Hernan Cortés arrived in Mexico. One story goes that the Aztecs thought he was their returning god, Quetzalcoatl, and gave him a royal welcome. Cortés and his army seized and destroyed Tenochtitlán, and Mexico fell under Spanish rule. Millions of Aztecs and other native peoples were killed in the invasion or by diseases brought by the Spanish.

This statue of Hernan Cortés is in Medellín, Spain, the city of his birth.

Rebellion

Civil-war revolutionaries like Emiliano Zapata became national heroes.

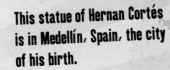

Spanish rule finally ended in 1821, after a rebellion and war that killed thousands. But following independence, Mexico's wealth stayed in the hands of just a few people. Eventually a revolution formed against the ruling dictator, Porfirio Díaz. Civil war raged for a decade from 1910. The outcome was a new Revolutionary Party that promised changes to help the poor.

About 30 per cent of today's Mexicans are indigenous, while 60 per cent are mestizo (part indigenous, part European).

Land of Extremes

It's dusty and dry in the north Mexican deserts, but dripping wet in the rainforests of the south! In Mexico you'll also find high mountains, deep canyons, pointy peninsulas and curving bays. It's a land of sunshine, snow and howling hurricanes. What's more, Mexico is right in line with the Pacific 'Ring of Fire' – one of the shakiest earthquake and volcano zones on the planet.

NO WAY!

The chihuahua (a tiny breed of dog that has been seen in ladies' handbags) is named after the north-Mexican state!

You can see how Popocatépetl, Aztec for 'Smoking mountain', got its name!

Ring of Fire

In 1943, a Mexican farmer got a big surprise when a volcano, Parícutin, appeared in his corn field! Mexico has plenty of other volcanoes, including the highly active Popocatépetl. The country is regularly rocked by earthquakes – a severe one in 1985 destroyed much of Mexico City. All this happens because Mexico lies at the junction of several tectonic plates.

The Sonoran Desert is the hottest in Mexico and home to the giant saguaro cactus.

High and Low

Mexico's highest peak is a dormant volcano, Pico de Orizaba, at 4,922m. It's set in the Sierra Madre Mountains – an extension of the US Rockies – which are made up of three smaller ranges. Between the mountains is a high and cool central plateau where most people in Mexico live. Swooping down to sea level, beach-lovers can enjoy a 9,330km coastline that borders two sides of the land.

Wet and Dry

If you're looking for a soaking, come to the Lacandon Jungle!

Huge and dry, the Chihuahuan Desert sprawls across the Mexico-United States border. It lies in the shadow of two mountain ranges, which block rain coming from the oceans. In contrast, the jungles of southern Mexico get up to 2,600mm of rainfall per year. The extreme wet weather feeds rivers and waterfalls, and attracts more plants and animals than you could hope to count.

City Living

BIG, BUSY and BOOMING are just three words that could describe Mexican cities! Since the Revolution, people have been flooding here from the countryside to find work. Now nearly four in five Mexicans live in urban areas. Many cities are a dizzying mix of soaring skyscrapers, ancient ruins, colonial palaces and tumbledown slums.

NO WAY!

Mexico City is sinking! So much water has been drained from the ground beneath it that the city drops by an estimated 10cm per year.

Great Guadalajara

Lively Guadalajara is about as Mexican as a city can get! The birthplace of mariachi music and the national drink tequila, it's also a key centre for business and industry. Over 4 million people live in the metropolitan area, among a patchwork of green parks, modern avenues, elegant buildings and colourful street art. You can hire a horse-drawn carriage to explore.

Admire the historic buildings of Mexico's second city, Guadalajara.

Tumbledown Town

Sometimes cities struggle to cope with a rush of immigrants from the countryside. Neza-Chalco-Itza in Mexico City is evidence of this – it's one of the world's biggest slums. About 4 million people live here in poor conditions, lacking electricity and clean water. Most squat illegally in makeshift homes, while others live in abandoned mansions that have become low-cost rental apartments.

A run-down building in Neza-Chalco-itza, Mexico City.

Colossal Capital

Once the site of the Aztec capital Tenochtitlán, Mexico City is now a hectic modern megalopolis! More than 20 million people live here, and it shows in the chockablock streets. Climb the Torre Latinoamericana to admire the city sprawl from 44 storeys high. Other attractions include the historic Zócalo square, an Aztec temple and people-watching in Alameda Park.

Mexico City is one of America's highest and oldest capitals.

Wonders of the World

If you like mysterious stories, you'll LOVE Mexico's ancient wonders! From abandoned cities to pyramid temples, they're stacked with secrets that go way back in time. Millions of tourists arrive each year to explore them, as well as the country's many other treasures. Join the crowds and let your imagination run wild...

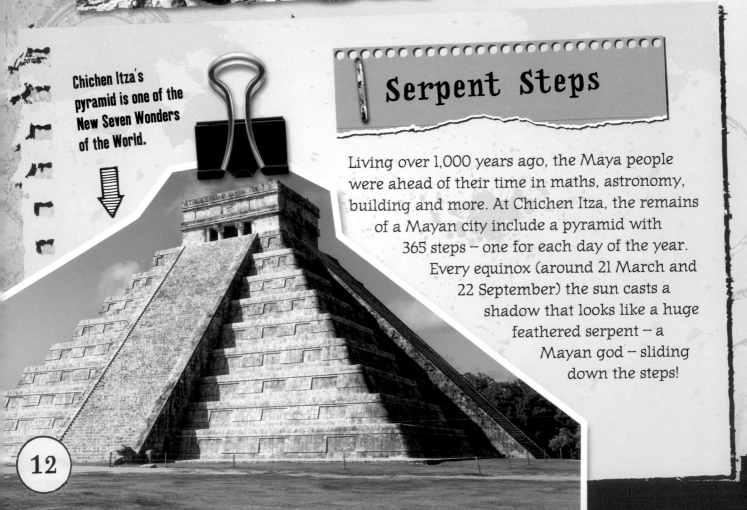

Chichen Itza's pyramid is one of the New Seven Wonders of the World.

Serpent Steps

Living over 1,000 years ago, the Maya people were ahead of their time in maths, astronomy, building and more. At Chichen Itza, the remains of a Mayan city include a pyramid with 365 steps – one for each day of the year. Every equinox (around 21 March and 22 September) the sun casts a shadow that looks like a huge feathered serpent – a Mayan god – sliding down the steps!

City of the Gods

Teotihuacan was massive – the first great city of the Americas – but no one really knows who built it! Flourishing between 100 and 650 CE, the 'city of the gods' was probably home to 100,000 people. The name comes from the Aztecs who, hundreds of years after the city was abandoned, adopted it as a sacred place. You can still see ancient palaces, pyramids and temples here.

You'll get fit walking round Teotihuacan!

NO WAY!

Nearly 24 million foreign tourists visited Mexico in 2013, generating US$13.8 billion!

Coastal Paradise

When your feet are tired from ancient exploring, why not relax on a white-sand beach! Holidays in Mexico can be an all-round adventure with a modern resort like Cancún as your base. The island of Cozumel, with its colourful coral reefs, is a popular diving and snorkelling spot. On the west coast you can nip down the remote Baja Peninsula and feel like you're in another world.

Cancún has over 20km of beaches and 240 days of sunshine per year!

Working the Land

Mexico is so big and its climate so varied that it's hard to find a crop that won't grow here. While agriculture isn't as big as it used to be, about one in seven Mexicans still farm the land. Many rural people grow food for their families, selling anything they have spare in local markets. It's a tough life, but if you like peace and quiet and aren't in a hurry, this is the place to be!

Traditional ways of sowing corn live on in parts of Mexico.

Corny Country

You'd have to walk around with your eyes closed to miss seeing maize (corn) in Mexico! This staple food was born here thousands of years ago, and is grown both on family plots and larger farms. Other top crops include fruits and vegetables – especially tomatoes, with over a million tonnes sold abroad every year. Mexico also produces huge volumes of sugar and coffee.

Meaty Market

Mexico is home to over 30 million cattle, 16 million pigs, 9 million goats and nearly 500 million chickens! It produces several million tonnes of beef, pork and poultry every year. The flip side is that Mexico has to import vast amounts of grain to use as animal feed. The country spends more on agricultural imports than it makes on equivalent exports.

Cows have plenty to eat in the lush southern state of Chiapas.

Rural Life

Rural Mexico is a world away from fast-paced city life. The villages of wood or mud houses don't have street signs or addresses. People cook on open fires, and while most now have electricity, there are still about a million without. Many families have just a small plot of land and struggle to eek out a living. At the other extreme, owners of large farms reap the benefits of modern machinery.

Fresh-from-the-farm produce goes on sale at a city market.

NO WAY!

Mexico exports more avocados, green peppers and limes than anywhere else in the world!

It's a Winner

It's safe to say that Mexicans are serious about sport. In ancient times, if you lost a ritual ball game you could be sacrificed to the gods! People here still put their lives on the line in dangerous bullfights and rodeos. But the most popular sport these days is football — at least 8 million Mexicans play it, and stadium audiences can reach a rip-roaring 100,000 fans on a big match day.

Football Mad!

Football pretty well paralyzes the country, especially when Mexico plays in a World Cup match! The national team has qualified 15 times and is one of the best in North America. It hovers in the top 20 FIFA world rankings and holds many titles, including the FIFA Confederations Cup and Pan American Games. In 2012, fans went mad when the team won gold at the London Olympics.

Mexican football fans display the colours of their national flag and favourite team.

Javier Hernández goes for a kick.

Traditional Sports

You might have seen the famous masks of Mexico's lucha libre wrestlers. These agile athletes fight in a series of scripted, choreographed moves. Another sport invented here is charrería – a rodeo event where charros (cowboys) in traditional costume compete in teams. Tests of their macho skills include riding wild horses and bulls, and catching the animals with a rope or lasso.

This masked 'luchador' means business!

Famous Players

Mexico's all-time top scorer was Jared Borgetti, who netted 46 goals before retiring in 2008. Today, striker Javier Hernández is the one to watch. Playing for Manchester United, he kicked 20 goals in his first season and is now on loan to Real Madrid. His jersey reads 'Chicharito', meaning 'little pea' – his dad was called 'Chicharo' (pea) because he had green eyes!

NO WAY!

Famous masked luchador El Santo ('The Saint') was a legend in Mexican sport. As well as wrestling for nearly 50 years, he appeared in many comic books and films!

On the Move

Mexico is a big country, but getting around it is no big deal. It has an amazing 1,714 airports — third only to the USA and Brazil. If you don't want to fly, take a long-distance bus down a multi-lane expressway, or cram into a colectivo (shared taxi). You can nip around town in a mototaxi (rickshaw) — or if you're deep in the countryside, jump on a burro (donkey)!

NO WAY!

The super-rich in Mexico City have taken to landing helicopters on the roofs of buildings to beat the traffic!

Scenic Railway

Passenger trains are few and far between in Mexico, but for the trip of a lifetime jump aboard the Copper Canyon Railway! Connecting the high, dry north to the Pacific coast, it passes jaw-dropping canyons, rushing waterfalls and dusty desert plains. Get ready to brave hairpin bends and dramatic trackside drops. The route covers 655km and crosses 36 bridges and 87 tunnels.

This train is not for the faint-hearted!

Beautiful Boats

Just an hour on the metro from the capital's chaotic centre, a very different scene awaits. Trajineras are colourful, gondola-like boats that cruise around a network of canals and floating garden islands. Developed in Aztec times, they're used by locals and tourists alike. There's a lively party atmosphere at weekends, with musicians and vendors paddling around in other boats.

You can rent a boat complete with food and musicians.

On Your Bike

In Mexico City, traffic is so slow at rush hour that cycling can be the best way from A to B. Ecobici is a government scheme that rents bikes around town, with about 25,000 trips made each day. The city also has 'no drive' days for certain vehicles, and the main street closes to cars on Sundays so that people can stroll traffic-free. All this is helping to change the image of 'smog city'.

 What, no gridlock? It must be Sunday!

Going Wild

If you're a keen wildlife spotter, pack your binoculars! Mexico is considered a 'megadiverse' country, meaning it's home to more species than most other places on Earth. Over 200,000 different types of plants and animals live here, including thousands of species that aren't found anywhere else. Mexico is also a hotbed for dinosaur fossils!

Every winter, millions of monarch butterflies travel up to 4,000km from the USA and Canada. Arriving at a special reserve in Mexico, they literally smother the tree trunks and branches!

Very small and very rare, the volcano rabbit lives only in Mexico – mainly on the slopes of four volcanoes.

NO WAY!

Apatosaurus was a giant, plant-eating dinosaur that lived in Mexico about 150 million years ago!

Grey whales swim all the way from the Arctic to breed in Mexico's warmer waters. They're often covered in barnacles, making them look like crusty ocean rocks.

The Old Man Cactus of eastern Mexico is so-named for its shaggy coat of silvery-white hair!

The Aztecs named their bravest fighters 'jaguar warriors' after a killer wildcat. The jaguar is a ferocious hunter, but highly endangered in Mexico.

Lively Life

Get ready to celebrate in Mexico! This is a country of warm, friendly people who put family and festivities first. Every religious, national or local holiday involves a party – and a party's not a party without a piñata. If you've ever hit a paper maché toy full of sweets and toys with a stick, you've played this popular Mexican game.

The Mexican tradition of piñata has spread around the world!

School Days

Schoolchildren in Mexico start their day singing the national anthem. Classes begin around 8am and include Spanish, English, maths, art and history. At 3pm, pupils go home for a late lunch before doing homework or chores. School age here is 6-16 – some children drop out early to work and support their families, but over 93 per cent of Mexicans aged 15 or over can now read and write.

In Mexico, 98 per cent of primary-aged children go to school.

Day of the Dead

It might sound spooky, but Mexicans believe that once a year the spirits of the dead return to Earth. On 1 November, children come, followed by adults on the 2nd. Mexicans treat this as a time to celebrate – to honour lost friends and relatives and not be afraid of death. They make and decorate ofrendas (altars) with food, flowers, photos and sugar skulls.

NO WAY!

Mexican children don't get presents on Christmas Day but on 6 January, when they celebrate the arrival of the Three Wise Men.

Fancy dress is a big part of Day of the Dead.

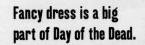

Catholic Nation

Most Mexicans are Roman Catholics – in fact they're the second-biggest Catholic nation after Brazil! Our Lady of Guadalupe in Mexico City is one of the world's most visited Catholic shrines. Pilgrims flock here in their thousands to pray, get a blessing or pin charms called milagros on the tunic of a figure of a saint, to ask for a favour or miracle.

On the Money

These are exciting times for Mexico. Its economy is growing fast and already ranks 11th in the world. But Mexico also has one of the widest gaps between rich and poor, and corruption and crime rates are high. The government faces the challenge of trying to spread wealth more fairly. After all, Mexicans come top in official figures for the hardest-working people on the planet!

Working Away

Many people seek their fortunes across the border in the USA. More than 11.5 million Mexicans have moved there, making them the USA's biggest immigrant group. Thousands more are arrested each month, trying to cross illegally. In 2013, Mexicans in the USA sent nearly US$22 billion home to their families. The only industry that brings in more foreign income is oil.

Workers in Mexico average 45 hours a week — more than any other industrialized nation.

Shopping plazas are springing up in Mexico's cities.

Bright Side

The top fifth of Mexicans earn 13 times more than the bottom fifth. However, Mexico's middle class is growing. An increasing number of people have been through education, got good jobs and have more money to spend. Owning homes, cars and computers, eating out and shopping for designer clothes are just a few things that are on the rise.

NO WAY!

Mexico's telecoms giant Carlos Slim is worth more than US$80 billion – the second-richest man in the world. Meanwhile, many Mexicans bring home less than $5 a day.

Factory Boom

Mexico does a lot of trade with the USA, thanks to the creation of NAFTA (the North American Free Trade Association). It shipped more than US$300 million of exports – mainly oil, vehicles and telecoms equipment – to the USA in 2013. US-owned factories called maquiladoras have sprung up along the border. Workers here make things like cars and TVs for low wages, using imported parts.

This factory makes steering wheels for an American car company.

Ready to Eat?

If you're used to eating early, prepare to be hungry in Mexico! Catching on from the Spanish, the Mexicans eat late – around 2-4pm for lunch, their main meal. Breakfast could be anything from a quick coffee to a huge spread including huevos rancheros (fried eggs on tortillas with a spicy tomato sauce). Dinner tends to be light – maybe soup or a plate of tacos.

NO WAY!

We have Mexico to thank for chocolate! People here were making drinks from cacao as early as 1900 BCE. The Aztecs even used cacao beans as currency.

Natural Spice

Mexican food is known for its spicy flavours. Chilli peppers are native to Mexico – one conquistador wrote that without chilli, the indigenous people didn't think they were eating! Mexican chillis come in many sizes, colours and strengths and crop up in almost every dish. Look out for eye-watering habaneros – some of the spiciest peppers around.

If you can't stand the heat, avoid the chillis!

Holy Mole

One story behind the Mexican sauce mole (mo-lay) tells of two nuns surprised by a visitor. Short of food, they ground up every ingredient they could find and simmered it in liquid. Today's mole sauces still contain loads of ingredients – from chilli and garlic to chocolate. Guacamole is different – a dip made from mashed-up avocado, often served alongside tomato salsa and refried beans.

 Moles come in different colours, from red like this one to black and green.

Five Ways with Tortillas

Tortillas are Mexican flatbreads made from cornmeal or flour. Here are just a few ways to eat them:

Taco

Taco – wrap a soft or fried tortilla around a filling (eg spicy grasshoppers if you're in Oaxaca)

Chilaquiles – lightly fry, cut into quarters and top with salsa, eggs and cheese (for breakfast)

Enchilada – roll around a filling, cover with a tomato-chilli sauce, then bake

Quesadilla – fill with cheese (and anything else you like), fold in half then cook

Tostada – deep-fry a flat (or stale) tortilla and add a topping

Quesadilla

Amazing Arts

Mexicans can make a masterpiece out of almost anything – carving stone, twisting silver, threading beads and even shaping sugar. Wherever you go, you'll find something different, from colourful indigenous weavings to paper maché dolls. The Mexican arts are full of fun and imagination. Just switch on the TV and you'll see it in their well-loved telenovelas (soap operas) too!

Festive Faces

For thousands of years, Mexicans have worn masks in dances, festivals and other rituals. Masks were believed to transform the wearer into whatever creature or god they showed. Usually handcrafted from wood (or sometimes coconuts!), today's masks are painted in bright colours.

This mask is made of painted clay.

NO WAY!

Every Christmas, Oaxaca has a festival to celebrate the radish. Craftsmen carve giant vegetables into human figures and other amazing shapes!

Local Talent

Every region in Mexico has its own artistic style. In the indigenous villages of Oaxaca you'll find colourful woven rugs, carved wooden animals and black pots. The state of Puebla is famous for its glazed ceramics called Talavera. If you like fancy beadwork, head to Jalisco.

Beadwork

Talavera

Double Act

Two great 20th-century Mexican artists, Diego Rivera and Frida Kahlo, were married, then divorced, then married again! Frida was famous for her intimate self-portraits, while Diego painted massive public murals that showed his views on Mexico's history and politics.

Rivera's mural, 'The History of Mexico'.

Hat Music

Put on a charro costume and a big sombrero hat, and you're ready to play mariachi! This Mexican folk music uses string instruments and often accompanies dancing. The Mexican Hat Dance is skippy and fast, while the zapateado involves so much foot-stamping that it has damaged floors!

A moustache isn't essential, but it's part of the mariachi look!

More Information

Websites

http://www.lonelyplanet.com/mexico
All you need to prepare for a trip to Mexico.

http://www.visitmexico.com
The Mexico Tourism official website.

https://www.cia.gov/library/publications/the-world-factbook/geos/mx.html
The CIA World Factbook Mexico page, with up-to-date info and statistics.

http://kids.nationalgeographic.com/explore/countries/mexico
An overview of Mexico for kids.

http://www.timeforkids.com/destination/mexico/sightseeing
An interactive guide, including tips on the Spanish language and a quiz.

Movies and TV

The Feathered Serpent (TV series on DVD, PG)
A 1970s children's series set in ancient Mexico.

Nacho Libre (12A)
A Mexican monk works up the courage to become a lucha libre wrestler!

Clips

http://www.bbc.co.uk/education/clips/z382hyc
An overview of Mexico's geography.

http://www.bbc.co.uk/education/clips/z4xfgk7
Mexico City, from Aztec to modern times.

http://www.bbc.co.uk/education/clips/zgwxn39
Life in rural Mexico.

http://www.bbc.co.uk/education/clips/zphpyrd
A series of clips on the Aztecs, from their history to customs.

https://www.youtube.com/watch?v=87Ttti3z4Tc
A Mexican Hat Dance performance.

Apps

Google Earth by Google, inc
Explore Mexico (and the rest of the world) from the sky – for free!

Mexico Travel Guide by Triposo
A bundle of background info, city guides, maps and phrasebooks.

Learn Spanish by Bravolol
Pick up the lingo from a Spanish-speaking parrot!

Mexican Food by Cupcake Kids inc
Learn some Mexican recipes in this interactive game.

Books

Food and Cooking Around the World: Mexico
by Rosemary Hankin (Wayland, 2015)
A World of Food: Mexico
by Geoff Barker (Franklin Watts, 2015)
The Ancient World: Ancient Maya
by Barbara A. Somervill (Scholastic, 2012)
Countries Around the World: Mexico
by Ali Brownlie (Raintree, 2011)
Horrible Histories: The Angry Aztecs
by Terry Deary (Scholastic, 2008)

Try making a piñata by decorating a cardboard box, filling it with sweets, then hanging it on a string ready to hit!

Glossary

astronomy The science of space objects including stars, moons and planets.

civilization An organized society with systems of government, culture, industry and so on.

civil war A war between people of the same country.

colonial Relating to a period of foreign rule, in this case the rule of Mexico by Spain.

conquistador One of the leaders of the Spanish conquest of Mexico in the 16th century.

coral reef A rock-like structure under the sea, made up of billions of organisms called coral polyps.

corruption Dishonest actions by people in positions of power.

dictator A ruler with total power over a country, usually gained by force.

immigrants People who arrive in a new place to live.

indigenous Native to a particular place.

megalopolis A very large, heavily populated city.

revolution The overthrow of a government by the people.

rodeo An event where cowboys show their skills at riding and roping wild horses and cattle.

rural Relating to the countryside, rather than towns.

slum An overcrowded urban area with very poor standards of living.

sombrero A wide-brimmed felt or straw hat.

tectonic plates Sections of Earth's crust, which fit together like a jigsaw and float on hot rock beneath.

tequila A famous alcoholic drink made in north-west Mexico from the blue agave plant.

Index